Baby and Beyond

Progression in Play for Babies and Children

Movement and Beat

Published 2009 by A&C Black Publishers Limited
36 Soho Square, London W1D 3QY
www.acblack.com

ISBN 978-1-4081-1246-5
Text © Clare Beswick 2009
Series Editor: Sally Featherstone Illustrations © Martha Hardy 2009

Printed in Great Britain by Latimer & Company Limited

This book is produced using paper that is made from wood grown in managed, sustainable forests. It is natural, renewable and recyclable.
The logging and manufacturing processes conform to the environmental regulations of the country of origin.

**To see our full range of titles
visit www.acblack.com**

Contents

Introduction

This book gives ideas for introducing and extending movement and beat activities for babies and young children. Each page spread contains a range of experiences and a selection of ideas for each of the developmental stages of the Early Years Foundation Stage (EYFS). Developmental stages 4, 5 and 6 have been combined over two sections:

0-11 months	8-20 months	16-26 months	22-40 months	40-60+ months
Developmental Stage 1	Developmental Stage 2	Developmental Stage 3	Developmental Stages 4 and 5	Developmental Stages 5 and 6

Movement and dance activities such as crawling, creeping, rolling, turning, walking, skipping, reaching, and swinging are essential for babies' and young children's brain development. These specific activities make full use of a baby's complicated nervous system and follow a plan. The nervous system of every baby needs to go through a series of developmental stages before the brain can operate at its full potential. In using their bodies, repeating sounds and movements, and using all their senses, babies and young children programme the learning machines we call their brains.

This process takes place between birth and around seven years of age, and the first year is critical. By twelve months, the brain has grown to 50 per cent of its adult size, and babies are well on their way to the walking, talking, thinking being that we recognise as an adult.

If babies do not have the opportunity to roll, crawl, creep, rock, turn, stretch, clasp, focus, babble, clap and do many more movements such as these, gaps in their development may appear in the years ahead. However, in the interest of love and safety, babies are sometimes kept off the floor for much of their first year. A baby who spends too much time being restrained in a car seat, stroller or baby chair, or being held or lying on a blanket on their back will not move through the important fundamental patterns of the first twelve months of life, developing their bodies and their brains.

Games, songs, nursery rhymes, music, movement, clapping and action rhymes are all familiar and traditionally recognised activities in the early years. We now know that these are not just enjoyable activities, but fundamental to building a strong, flexible, responsive brain in a well co-ordinated body. Rhymes and rhythm sharpen listening skills and support phonological awareness, essential to speaking, reading and writing. Action and movement songs help co-ordination by using both sides of the brain, and dancing, movement, playing simple instruments and beat work all reinforce those essential links between brain cells.

Of course, in previous generations, babies and children sang and played these games at home, within their family. Provision of universal daycare for under fives has transferred the responsibility for early rhythm and beat work to practitioners and early years settings. The guidance for the Early Years Foundation Stage in England strongly emphasises the need for practitioners to make time for these early language and learning activities.

A strong and wide repertoire of nursery songs, rhymes and action games, supported by movement to beat and a range of different sorts of music, will help you to engage and enhance children's enjoyment of movement activities with other children and adults. This enjoyment will be increased if the adults join in, modelling and participating in the activities with the children. By starting with the youngest babies and involving them in simple songs and games you will ensure that you are making a big difference to every child's development.

Young babies (0-11 months)	Babies (8-20 months)	Young children (16-26 months)	Children (22-40 months)	Older children (40-60+ months)

Developmental Stage 1	Developmental Stage 2	Developmental Stage 3	Developmental Stages 4 & 5	Developmental Stages 5 & 6

Rhythms of Life

Making sounds and rhythms are instinctive behaviours for humans, both adults and children. Any object, whether it is made for music or not can help you to enjoy rhythm and beat with babies and children every day. Household utensils, simple objects, anything handy will do for these informal moments.

Young babies (0-11 months)

As you are caring for babies, draw their attention to the small sounds you can make with familiar objects. Tap on a tin with a spoon as you prepare their feed, tickle them gently and rhythmically as you change them – a spoon on a plate, a toy gently banged on a table, a tap running will all draw attention. As babies begin to make sounds themselves, tape their first gurglings and cooings and play them back to them. Watch what happens!

Developmental Stage 1

Babies (8-20 months)

Older babies will love to play tapping and banging games with you or on their own. Add lots of objects to tap, shake, rattle and bang to your treasure baskets. Metal objects are good, as are small containers with a few even smaller items safely trapped inside, for waving and shaking. Offer rattles of all sorts, and join babies as they play with them, encouraging rhythmic shaking and banging. A saucepan and wooden spoon will give hours of fun.

Developmental Stage 2

Young children (16-26 months)

Wooden spoons, chopsticks, or just short sticks from the garden can be added to plastic or meta containers, such as empty plastic boxes or biscuit tins, for banging and tapping. The outdoors is a good place for such noisy activities! When you go on walks and short visits, explore sounds you can make in the environment – tapping and banging on fences, railings, park benches and drain covers. Listen to the different sounds and patterns you can make together.

Developmental Stage 3

Children (22-40 months)

Hang metal objects such as saucepans, frying pans and large metal spoons to a fence or bush, and offer children drumsticks or more spoons to tap and bang them with. Use home-made instruments such as shakers, rattles, sticks and tins to accompany your story times, making sound effects for footsteps, running, doors banging, rain or thunder. Leave the instruments where children can get them to accompany their own play and stories.

Developmental Stages 4 & 5

Older children (40-60+ months)

Visit a 'Pound Shop' and buy some cheap washing-up bowls and buckets. Make some drumsticks by binding fabric round the end of short dowels or chopsticks. Turn the buckets and bowls upside down for a cheap and versatile drum set that the children will really enjoy using. Provide a basket of home-made musical instruments, such as pairs of sticks or metal spoons, bells, rattles, 'rain' sticks – put dried peas or pasta in cardboard or plastic tubes and seal the ends.

Developmental Stages 5 & 6

Clapping

Clapping is central to beat work and gaining a sense of rhythm. Encourage babies and children to clap along, even when they need you to gently hold their hands to make sure they actually meet. Clap along to rhymes, songs, music and poetry, so they get a real sense of the beat of language.

Young babies (0-11 months)

Model clapping as soon as babies can focus on you and your hands. Young babies will need to be near you, and you should keep your hands near your face, but not covering it, so the baby can see both your face and your hands. Clap rhythmically as you talk to the baby, or sing simple songs or chant rhymes. Introduce some simple clapping games and rhymes such as 'Pat-a-Cake', or clap along to other nursery rhymes or the radio.

Developmental Stage 1

Babies (8-20 months)

Once they can sit up unaided, babies love any game that involves clapping or patting. You may have to gently hold their hands to start with, until they can make them meet unaided. Clapping is the way most babies use to show their enjoyment and general happiness, and they love being encouraged to do it again and again. You can play clapping games either face to face or with the baby on your lap, facing away, as you hold their hands.

Developmental Stage 2

Young children (16-26 months)

Clapping helps co-ordination and is a great way to keep small hands busy while you sing at group times. As children expand their vocabulary, you can support this by teaching them lots of simple rhymes, and clapping along as you sing or say them. You could get a nursery rhyme anthology or collect your own by asking colleagues, families of the children, your own friends and your family. Add rhymes that reflect the cultures and backgrounds of the children.

Developmental Stage 3

Children (22-40 months)

Get in the habit of clapping everywhere – when you walk to another room, when you are clearing up, while you wait for food or snacks. Do clapping rhymes several times every day, as this will really help fine motor development and listening. Make up some silly clapping rhymes – children at this age love them. Use rhyming or nonsense words such as *'Clap, clap, clap; Tap, tap, tap; Flap, flap, flap; Snap, snap, snap.'*

Developmental Stages 4 & 5

Older children (40-60+ months)

Keep introducing new songs and rhymes and make up your own together. Play some clapping games such as *'If You're Happy...'* in pairs, but make sure it's an enjoyable activity for everyone. As children get used to clapping, try singing some familiar clapping songs as you move the clapping from one side of the body to the other. *'Clap, clap here; Clap, clap there; Clap, clap high; Clap, clap low'* is a really good way of making bodies and brains work a bit harder.

Developmental Stages 5 & 6

Stamping and Slapping

Stamping extends the beat work you have already established through clapping. The sound of new or different shoes will give an emphasis and interest to the activity, and adding other movements such as slapping, or some simple instruments will ensure continuing interest and challenge.

Young babies (0-11 months)

A good way to sensitise babies to movement and beat is to use a steady beat yourself as you carry them. Stamp or walk slowly and rhythmically round the setting, or as you visit the garden or the shops. Gently add some slaps to your thighs or their legs as you say and sing rhymes together. As babies gradually become aware of their own bodies, encourage them to gently stamp their own feet as you hold them under their arms.

Developmental Stage 1

Babies (8-20 months)

Thigh slapping is a simple and natural movement for babies as they get involved in and excited by learning. Mirror their movements by doing them yourself, slapping and clapping together. As they get more mobile, babies will love slapping and patting – make some 'pat mats' from zip-lock bags, part filled with shaving foam, cornflour and water, paste with glitter added, or thick paint. Use these to encourage rhythmical patting with both hands (or feet!).

Developmental Stage 2

Young children (16-26 months)

Stamping in mud, puddles, paint or compost is a great way of getting rid of energy as the children learn to manage their legs and feet. Put an old towel in the bottom of the tray to reduce slipping, and stay close. Add thigh slapping and stamping to circle time songs and rhymes, but keep the rhythm simple, so the children can keep time as they change from 'slap' to 'clap' and from 'clap' to 'stamp'. Stamping round the play area together is great fun!

Developmental Stage 3

Children (22-40 months)

Use stamping as an alternative to clapping as you share rhymes. Make up simple rhythms such as '*Stamp, stamp, stamp; Clap, clap, clap; Stamp, stamp; Clap, clap; Stamp, stamp, stamp.*' Adapt movement songs such as '*Wind the Bobbin*' by adding stamping ad clapping to the winding and pointing. Play '*Follow Me*' by making a simple rhythm yourself for them to copy, such as '*Clap, clap, slap*' or '*Stamp, stamp, clap, clap.*'

Developmental Stages 4 & 5

Older children (40-60+ months)

As older children get used to the movements, let them challenge each other at group time, by making up short movement rhymes for other children to copy, using clapping, slapping and stamping. Add stamping to your movement rhymes by adapting songs such as 'Old MacDonald' to:
'*Old MacDonald had a gym, EIEIO,
And in that gym we learn to stamp, EIEIO,
With a stamp, stamp here, stamp, stamp there, Here a stamp, there a stamp, everywhere a stamp, stamp...*'

Developmental Stages 5 & 6

Marching

Marching is a co-ordinated action where hands, arms, body and legs are moving together in rhythm, with opposite arms matching each step. This cross-body movement is an important way of building links between the two sides of the brain to extend physical and thinking power.

Young babies (0-11 months)

Get babies used to the marching rhythm by marching yourself as you carry them. Or use an empty box, a saucepan or tin as a drum to march to. Exaggerated movement helps babies to feel your movement through their bodies. Sing rhymes with marching rhythms such as 'The Grand Old Duke of York' or 'The Ants go Marching' or just march to upbeat songs on the radio.

Developmental Stage 1

Babies (8-20 months)

Drums make a good accompaniment to marching, and babies love bashing simple drums. Record or download some band music and play it in your setting for a good rhythm time with home made drums made from empty boxes or tins. Hold hands with standing babies and march on the spot with them – using one foot then the other is good practice for walking, and exercises both sides of the brain and the body.

Developmental Stage 2

Young children (16-26 months)

Marching in the garden is a good activity for lively children at this stage of development. Join them in some marching by bringing some instruments or flags outside and having a parade or procession. Or sing marching songs as you parade around. 'Soldier' marching, with arms swinging at their sides, will help children to co-ordinate opposite arms and feet in a real marching movement which exercises both sides of the brain.

Developmental Stage 3

Children (22-40 months)

Try playing some marching music to help children focus when it's clearing up time. It really helps some children. You could also march to snack, to lunch or to a special activity. Use recorded marching music to invigorate children when they need to let off steam or after sitting still. Marching in and out of a group in a clear space is very good for developing spatial awareness as children try to avoid bumping into each other.

Developmental Stages 4 & 5

Older children (40-60+ months)

A different version of 'The Grand Old Duke of York' requires children to bend and stretch their legs as they go up the hill and down again. Marching with a partner, or in a line of three makes this more demanding, especially if the children are following a line or marching to music. Add rattles, shakers, drums and other instruments to play as you march. This makes it more fun AND more challenging for everyone. Or try clapping as you march – another challenging activity.

Developmental Stages 5 & 6

Waving and Wrapping

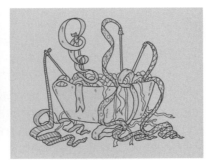

Waving simple ribbon sticks, chopsticks, feathers, flowers or other objects in their hands will help babies and children to co-ordinate left and right hands and arms, and to focus their eyes on their hands. This 'conducting' to rhymes and music is a good way of helping to establish beat and rhythm.

Young babies (0-11 months)

Help tiny babies to focus by gently and slowly waving a stick with a feather, bell or flower on the end. Remember, babies need to be close (about 20cm from the object) to be able to focus, but make sure objects are safe for those lightning grabbing fingers! Rhythmically moving objects such as clock pendulums and rocking toys will fascinate some babies. Once their grasp has developed, try some safe, soft rattles to wave.

Developmental Stage 1

Babies (8-20 months)

Wrist rattles are fun, on either wrists or ankles, and will encourage babies to move their arms and legs to make the sounds. Waving rattles and other toys on sticks will help with control and hand/eye co-ordination. Add sound makers and wavers to your treasure baskets – try balls and bricks with bells inside, little tins or transparent plastic boxes filled with buttons or beads, artificial flowers on safe stalks and shakers of all sorts.

Developmental Stage 2

Young children (16-26 months)

You can introduce ribbon sticks at this stage, but you will need to supervise them carefully to avoid accidents. Ribbons or fabric strips tied to fingers, wrists and arms are safer and just as much fun. Make them in lots of colours so they appeal to boys as well as girls. Stretchy fabrics such as Lycra are great fun for wrapping, pulling and stretching. Children love wrapping themselves in it and pushing against the stretchiness to 'escape'.

Developmental Stage 3

Children (22-40 months)

Small group parachute games with some squares of stretchy fabric, such as Lycra, will give plenty of opportunities to work together and strengthen hands and fingers. Try making some stretchy fabric into 'body sacks' like pillow cases, that children can get right inside. Then they can stretch and move the fabric from inside, using muscles and limbs safely in a new activity. Make superhero cloaks to encourage running with out-stretched arms.

Developmental Stages 4 & 5

Older children (40-60+ months)

At this stage, ribbon sticks can be used to reinforce fine motor skills of letter and number formation by making it a whole body experience. Flags and streamers also liven up parades and processions for birthdays, celebrations or just for fun. Make some huge flags from lightweight fabrics on long bamboo canes and practise swirling and swooping the giant flags. Offer children Lycra or other stretchy materials for play which strengthens their muscles.

Developmental Stages 5 & 6

Keeping Still!

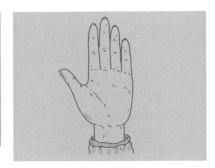

Stopping, pausing, waiting and anticipating all have to be learned, and music, rhymes and simple instruments will offer plenty of enjoyable practice for children at all stages of development. Musical games are a good way of extending the experiences for older children.

Young babies (0-11 months)

When you talk to and play with young babies, practise the exaggerated pause and gasp before a surprise or revealing a familiar or new object. Pausing and holding the body still needs good muscle control, and this needs practice and an understanding of when quietness and stillness are appropriate. Make sure you have plenty of quiet times with your key children, when you can appreciate the stillness together.

Developmental Stage 1

Babies (8-20 months)

Babies love surprises and surprise toys, so make sure you have plenty of these to share with sitting and standing babies. Pop-up toys, Jack-in-the-box, sucker and spring toys and toy toasters, will all give babies opportunities to wait and watch for the surprise. They will want these games and toys again and again. Moving towards them, then staying still (with or without a favourite toy) is another game that will intrigue them.

Developmental Stage 2

Young children (16-26 months)

Moving (running, walking, crawling) and stopping in a big space will help young children to get the control of their bodies that they need for keeping still. Lots of enjoyable short activities such as being a Jack-in-the-box, a frog, a chick hatching or a seed growing will also help. Children love surprises and being the loud noise – practise singing or saying short rhymes and songs in a whisper, then in a shout. Make tiny and HUGE movements, LOUD and soft sounds.

Developmental Stage 3

Children (22-40 months)

Play plenty of games where children need to be still and quiet, such as *'Statues'* or *'Dead Lions'*. Some songs, such as *'Dingle Dangle Scarecrow'* have loud and soft verses which can help children to recognise what is happening to their voices and bodies at different volumes. Stopping and starting games and activities will help them to control their bodies and voices. Try 'Stop, Start' races, bike rides, stories and rhymes.

Developmental Stages 4 & 5

Older children (40-60+ months)

As children get older, they can manage all sorts of 'Missing Word' or 'Missing Action' games such as *'What's the Time Mr Wolf?'* or *'Chinese Whispers'* and songs such as *'Heads, Shoulders, Knees and Toes'*, *'Ten Fat Sausages'* or *'In a Cottage in a Wood'* where the song loses a word or substitutes an action each time you repeat it. Stopping and starting when playing a musical instrument is a key skill which needs teaching and practice, starting at this age.

Developmental Stages 5 & 6

Rhymes with Actions

All children love action songs and rhymes, so try to have plenty in your personal collection. Frequent practice in moving to rhymes and words, as well as to songs, really helps with the key skills of listening, speaking and reading, so make sure you include them every day, and encourage parents to do so too.

Young babies (0-11 months)

Babies love to see you and hear you talking and singing just for them, so start young with movement rhymes and simple songs. '*This Little Piggy (or mouse) Went to Market*', '*This Little Cow Eats Grass*', '*Round and Round the Garden*', '*Two Little Dickey Birds*' and many others can be found in Nursery Rhyme collections or on the Internet. Use these regularly (ideally every day) so babies get used to the movements and the words by seeing and hearing you.

Developmental Stage 1

Babies (8-20 months)

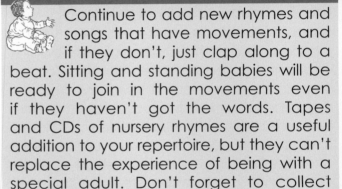

Continue to add new rhymes and songs that have movements, and if they don't, just clap along to a beat. Sitting and standing babies will be ready to join in the movements even if they haven't got the words. Tapes and CDs of nursery rhymes are a useful addition to your repertoire, but they can't replace the experience of being with a special adult. Don't forget to collect some local rhymes and those from different countries and cultures.

Developmental Stage 2

Young children (16-26 months)

Young children are enthusiastic about all sorts of movement songs and rhymes, starting with old favourites such as *'Twinkle, Twinkle, Little Star'*. Choose versions that have simple, whole body movements, and add some with hand and finger movements to help strengthen fingers and thumbs. Taking turns in counting songs such as *'Five Brown Buns'* or *'Five Speckled Frogs'* are useful, but should be done in small groups so everyone has a go.

Developmental Stage 3

Children (22-40 months)

Begin to add to songs and rhymes some more complex sequences of movements such as *'I'm a Little Teapot'*, *'Miss Polly'* or *'The Wheels on the Bus'* and add some extra verses to the ones they enjoy. Keep adding to the repertoire of songs n your setting, so the children have a wide range of physical experiences. Have a singing and movement session out of doors where you can sing as loud as you like and move with freedom in the fresh air.

Developmental Stages 4 & 5

Older children (40-60+ months)

Use some of the children's favourite rhymes to make up new versions, using characters from stories, TV and film. You could try *'Spiderman, Spiderman, Fly Away Home'* or *'Barbie, Barbie, Quite Contrary'*. Use animal songs such as *'Daddy's Taking us to the Zoo'* to encourage animal movements. Keep adding finger and hand rhymes such as *'One Finger, One Thumb'*, *'Peter Hammers'* and *'Tommy Thumb'*. These will help with fine motor skills.

Developmental Stages 5 & 6

Using Music

A collection of music on CD is an essential resource for the early years. Try to expand the collection by choosing music of all sorts, all styles, from all cultures and countries. Teach children how to use a CD player as soon as they are able, so they can choose and play music during child-initiated play in your music area or out of doors.

Young babies (0-11 months)

Having music on in your setting is a good idea, but NOT if it becomes wallpaper! Choose the music carefully, and if you sometimes have a radio on in the background, make sure it is not intrusive and includes different sorts of music from various stations, even if it is not your favourite style. Sometimes just sit together and listen to some music, echoing the beat by waving or tapping your fingers, and singing or humming along.

Developmental Stage 1

Babies (8-20 months)

Musical toys are common for this age – pressing buttons and making the music play is part of the fun. Try and find some simple music players suitable for this age, and add some of the bedtime soothing toys. Encourage babies to wave, clap and sway in time to the music, or provide some simple instruments in a basket, so they can play along. Favourite music CDs begin to emerge at this age, and babies will often indicate that they need the same one again and again.

Developmental Stage 2

Young children (16-26 months)

At this stage, you can begin to teach young children how to use very simple CD players, so they can choose and play their own favourite music, stories and songs. Check and select carefully to make sure the players are sturdy and safe for the very young children. Music from the radio or from the CDs you have chosen will add to the experiences of listening to music. Try offering some music or a radio in the role play area or outside.

Developmental Stage 3

Children (22-40 months)

Children will love to bring their favourite music CDs from home to share with friends and practitioners. Enjoy this music at snack and group times as well as leaving time for them to explore the music with friends. When you offer or play music in your setting, make sure you vary the types and styles, so children get experiences of classical, pop, world music, jazz and all the other varieties. Playing, moving and singing along will add to the pleasure.

Developmental Stages 4 & 5

Older children (40-60+ months)

Create a music area in your setting, with dressing up clothes, music on CD and musical instruments to explore. Add a radio and open the area for free play and creativity. It is very useful to observe what goes on in this area, because some children will show you a very different side to their behaviour and learning. Provide some real or home-made microphones for karaoke play and singing indoors or in your garden.

Developmental Stages 5 & 6

Dancing

Most children will dance spontaneously, and carry on with dancing as long as we encourage and accept it. Make sure there are spaces, times and opportunities for dancing together, alone and with friends, and that children have plenty of music, instruments, fabrics and accessories for dancing.

Young babies (0-11 months)

Dancing with tiny babies is a good way to calm them and form a good first relationship. As you hold and talk to babies, move gently in a rhythmical way, swaying and even gently swooping up and down. You can even dance sitting down, singing along, listening to the radio or your favourite CD. Add a wrist rattle or shaker and this will engage the baby's attention too. Don't get embarrassed, this is an important activity and the baby will love it!

Developmental Stage 1

Babies (8-20 months)

Once babies can sit up and stand, they often move spontaneously to music, swaying and jiggling and bending their knees to familiar rhythms. Ask parents and carers about current favourites and whether you can borrow or record these to play for your key children. Dancing with a sitting or standing baby is good fun for all, holding hands and moving your bodies rhythmically, or waving and shaking simple musical instruments such as bell sticks, simple shakers or rattles.

Developmental Stage 2

Young children (16-26 months)

At this stage, young children will often sing and do little dances as they play. Offer them some simple resources for dancing, and make sure there are opportunities to dance indoors and outside. Giving a lead yourself will often spark their interest in a circle dance, some jiggling to pop music, or a response to strong rhythms in African or other world music. Scarves and ribbons will enhance their dances as they wave and swirl around.

Developmental Stage 3

Children (22-40 months)

A dancing area is a great idea for children of this age. Space, some music and some simple clothing, such as hats, capes, headbands or just pieces of fabric to wrap themselves in will be used enthusiastically as long as you give the time and your approval. Remember, boys and girls may be switched on to dancing by different sorts of resources, instruments and music, so provide a good range for them to choose from.

Developmental Stages 4 & 5

Older children (40-60+ months)

Space and time, both indoors and outside are essential if older children are to sustain their interest in dance and dancing. Make sure there are plenty of models for different sorts of dancing, from pop to ballet, modern dance, ballroom dancing, break dancing, salsa etc. Find out what the children know about dancing and provide support with clothing and accessories for different types. Ask some dancers to come and demonstrate for the children.

Developmental Stages 5 & 6

Swing, Sway and Rock

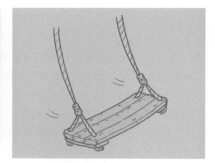

Swinging, swaying and rocking are all brain developing activities, but current safety concerns mean that rocking horses, swings and other such equipment is less available to young children. Try to build in some of these activities and find ways of providing swings, hammocks and other rocking experiences.

Young babies (0-11 months)

As you take a walk with a baby, perhaps one of your key children, walk with a swaying, swinging rhythm. It is now evident that singing and swaying actually help babies' and children's brains to develop, by stimulating brain cells. Sit together in a rocking chair, rock babies gently in your arms, sway as you talk to them face to face. Rocking cots and baby chairs are not only comforting but helpful in stimulating baby brains.

Developmental Stage 1

Babies (8-20 months)

Sit opposite older babies, or hold them facing you in your lap, and gently play swinging and rocking games such as 'Row the Boat', or swing them gently in a stretchy piece of fabric, suspended safely in your hands or between two adults. Once babies are mobile, safe rocking toys and rocking horses are very popular toys, and will encourage development of core body muscles as well as brain cells. Hammocks and simple baby swings are also favourites for all babies.

Developmental Stage 2

Young children (16-26 months)

Swinging has always been a great childhood activity, and swings are very popular with young children, but need careful supervision. It is better to just provide a simple rope to swing from, twisting round and spinning back. Make sure you do lots of swinging, swooping and swaying actions to music as you move and dance together, or sing songs such as 'Rock-a-bye-baby' or 'Dance to your Daddy' or try www.kididdles.com for some new lullabies.

Developmental Stage 3

Children (22-40 months)

Brahms' Lullaby is a popular piece for slow, gentle movement that children can follow in movement. Continue to play and sing 'Row the Boat' in pairs, and use ribbon sticks and chiffon scarves to encourage slow, gentle, swaying movement in groups or as part of your music and dance corner. Remember the different responses children will have if you vary the music for clearing up or group times, sometimes swinging and swaying as you come together.

Developmental Stages 4 & 5

Older children (40-60+ months)

Taking movements across the body makes the brain work harder, so continue to explore slow, rhythmic swinging. Teach some simple exercises such as drawing a big figure of eight on its side in the air; or being elephants, swinging from side to side with arms going down to the floor and up again to shoulder height, while you play some gently swinging music. Gentle swinging round and round on a single rope swing is also very good for stimulating the brain!

Developmental Stages 5 & 6

In a Circle

Beat songs and games in circles will help children to respond to others, and watch faces and bodies carefully. Listening skills are also supported when children can see each others' faces. Collect some circle songs and ring games, but remember that any song or rhyme can be converted into a circle game or dance.

Young babies (0-11 months)

Babies will really love sitting with you in a small circle with other babies, each with their own adult. Use these times to sing and talk, or share nursery rhymes. Passing an object round the group will get babies used to taking turns and sharing objects in a group, even when you have to hold the object for them. Remember, young babies need objects to be nearer than older babies do, as their focus is not well developed yet – 20cm is about right.

Developmental Stage 1

Babies (8-20 months)

Sitting babies will enjoy being able to see each other, and loose circles are ideal for many activities. Working with treasure baskets or other heuristic play materials will feel really companionable done where babies can watch each other, while having their own collection to explore. Sit with the babies as they work, establishing the circle as a good place to be, and an important place for you as well. Singing and rhyme time is another time for circles, as babies get used to being social.

Developmental Stage 2

Young children (16-26 months)

Passing objects round a circle is a good way to maintain attention, as long as the circle is not too big. Begin to establish a greeting time by saying hello to each child in turn, rolling a ball to them and back again as you greet each one, to keep their attention. Begin simple circle games at this stage, include ones where the children sit and one moves round (such as 'Duck, Duck, Goose'), and games where everyone is involved (such as Ring-a-Roses).

Developmental Stage 3

Children (22-40 months)

Continue to add circle games and songs to your repertoire. Moving round in a circle stimulates body and brain, and joining hands gives a real sense of community. Try working in two smaller circles, so children feel more secure, and make sure you play circle games out of doors as well as inside. 'The Okey Kokey', 'Sandy Girl', 'Here we go Round the Mulberry Bush', and 'Looby Lou' will all become firm favourites with their simple tunes and lots of movement.

Developmental Stages 4 & 5

Older children (40-60+ months)

Story rhymes are favourites with older children – 'The Princess', 'The Farmer's in His Den' 'In and Out the Dusty Bluebells', or 'I Sent a Letter to my Love' can be added to the repertoire. Ask families if they can remember any, and collect local or multicultural versions to share. A big band of stretchy material, such as lycra, is a good addition to circle times. If you thread a bracelet on it before you join the ends, children can all hold the band and slide the bracelet round to take a turn.

Developmental Stages 5 & 6

Hop, Skip and Jump

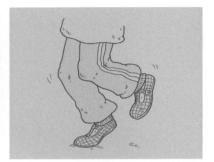

Simple jumping can start before babies can even hold themselves up – as long as they have a supportive adult to help them. Hopping and skipping are advanced skills for young children and they often need systematic teaching, but, once mastered, they contribute significantly to development.

Young babies (0-11 months)

As you play with your key group of babies, you will naturally lift them up so their feet are resting on your knee or on the floor. Babies will naturally move their feet in a 'walking' movement long before they can take any weight on their legs. Let them feel different textures and temperatures of surfaces as they sense them through bare feet. Give babies time for kicking when lying down. Help them to kick their legs, both together and one at a time, as you tickle their skin.

Developmental Stage 1

Babies (8-20 months)

Babies need plenty of time and space as they start to move under their own steam. Many will make the step from sitting or crawling to walking by holding their arms up to you for help. Hold them gently and let them feel the floor or grass under their feet as they start to develop their leg and foot muscles. Flat floors help with foot development, and many babies need lots of standing experience before they can transfer weight from one foot to another in walking.

Developmental Stage 2

Young children (16-26 months)

During the toddler stage, young children need plenty of practice in shifting their weight from one foot to another, and in moving with both feet together. Small changes in level, such as that between a carpet and the floor, can present a challenge that they will repeat over and over again, carefully stepping or 'jumping' over the join. Puddles, drain covers, steps, slopes and stairs are fascinating as children explore and become more adventurous jumpers and hoppers.

Developmental Stage 3

Children (22-40 months)

Simply going for a walk with this age group will become an adventure in the many ways they can use their bodies. It's a good idea to build this sort of movement into your walks and outings, playing simple versions of 'Follow the Leader' and 'Simon Says'. Hopping and jumping with both feet need plenty of practice, so give them some lines, circles and other shapes to follow by using chalk, paint or masking tape indoors and outside.

Developmental Stages 4 & 5

Older children (40-60+ months)

Older children are really beginning to get their bodies in control, but they still need plenty of opportunities to move and let off steam. Play lots of movement games that involve really thinking about fingers, arms, shoulders, legs, toes etc. Use descriptive words such as spin, twist, hop, turn, to describe movements, and add star jumps and bunny hops to their repertoire. Skipping (without a rope) needs help as it involves learning to hop on alternate feet!

Developmental Stages 5 & 6

Body Rhythms

Making music with your body by rhythmical tapping, slapping, popping, slapping, clicking is not only great fun but really supports cross brain activity and the development of gross and fine-motor skills. Help babies and children to explore what they can do to make body music alone or with a friend.

Young babies (0-11 months)

The beginnings of speech include lots of body language – blowing bubbles, gurgling, waving, slapping, kicking. Don't forget to notice and respond to this language – your response will encourage the baby to do more. Use some body language yourself – clapping, tapping, finger popping and clicking, whistling, gently blowing on their skin – these will all attract attention and make babies notice what you are doing when you are with them.

Developmental Stage 1

Babies (8-20 months)

At this stage clapping, flapping, kicking and cooing are used alongside their earliest words. Clapping is key, and 'Pat-a-Cake' will soon become a firm favourite. Exploring banging and patting hands on different surfaces (such as the floor, the tray of a high chair, the carpet, a wet table, a trail of spilt food) all give babies a sense of sound and texture. Feeling and patting their hair, your face or a simple 'pat mat' in a zip-lock bag are all experiences in sound discrimination.

Developmental Stage 2

Young children (16-26 months)

Simple songs with body sounds are important at this stage. The free instruments provided by their bodies are an instant accompaniment to songs and rhymes. Add some more movements such as slapping thighs, tapping cheeks, patting tummies to the more familiar clapping. Sing songs such as 'Peter Plays With one Hammer' or 'Old MacDonald' and make up your own rhymes or stories, using body sounds to accompany them.

Developmental Stage 3

Children (22-40 months)

Play simple games of 'I say, you say, I do, you do', where you say 'Clap, clap, slap' or 'Slap, slap, stamp' and they copy. Don't make the sequences too complicated. Tell simple sound stories where the children provide the sound track with body sounds. A simple story about a character getting up, yawning, cleaning their teeth, eating cereal, getting dressed, running down the stairs, going out and slamming the front door, will extend the fun.

Developmental Stages 4 & 5

Older children (40-60+ months)

Play sound copying games in a circle by 'passing' a body sound or simple pattern round the circle from one child to another. Sing sound songs such as 'We Can Play on the Big Bass Drum' or 'Daddy's Taking us to the Zoo Tomorrow' with plenty of body sounds. Tell more complex stories or add sounds to the ones you read, by inviting the children to invent sounds using their voices, bodies and simple instruments. Explore clicking, tapping, mouth popping etc.

Developmental Stages 5 & 6

I Say, You Say, I Do, You Do

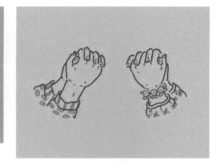

Copying movements is a good way to develop beat and co-ordination. Use songs and stories to practise 'I say, you say, I do, you do' in words, movement and song. As children get used to these sorts of games, they will love being challenged with strings of words or movements, and will even challenge you to follow them.

Young babies (0-11 months)

The instinct to copy facial expressions appears to be present at birth, and even newborn babies seem to be able to copy the expressions of the adults they see, as long as they have time to work on the muscles of their faces. Begin simple copying games by copying the expressions, sounds and movements babies make when you are with them. Babble back to them, copy their surprised, puzzled and happy expressions, and you will be rewarded by smiles!

Developmental Stage 1

Babies (8-20 months)

As soon as they realise they are separate people, babies seem to need to give things to others. Crawling and toddling babies will spend hours bringing things to an adult and dumping them in their lap. Build on this by playing passing games with babies, passing objects to and fro between you. Add to this game by playing with a hat or a pair of sunglasses, putting items on yourself and letting the baby tip or push them off. Many babies will play for ages like this.

Developmental Stage 2

Young children (16-26 months)

Copying each other is a good way to learn. Sit with children, and play simple games such as taking turns to post a shape into a postbox, drop a brick into a tin, put a plastic cup on a pile, clip a clothes peg round the edge of a tin or tap a tune on a tin or drum. Make faces at each other in a mirror or take turns to make a mark with paint or chalk. Roll out some dough or pastry and take turns cutting out shapes or fill paper cake cases with beads or pasta shapes.

Developmental Stage 3

Children (22-40 months)

'Follow Me' and 'Simon Says' are popular at this stage. Add to the fun by collecting lots of simple songs, rhymes and raps that can be used as following games. Beat Baby, Keeping the Beat CDs, and Beat Baby Raps from www.educationalpublications.com are all good resources for this sort of activity. Encouraging children to look at you and listen carefully will really help them with early literacy as well as supporting their physical development.

Developmental Stages 4 & 5

Older children (40-60+ months)

As children get better at these games, they can begin to lead them, while others (including the adults) can follow. Children love raps and as they get used to doing them, you can make some up together. Vary familiar games by playing 'Superman Says...' or use current favourite characters from TV or stories. Expand 'Put Your Finger on your Nose' by using strings of movements such as 'Put your finger on your nose, your elbow on your knee and your foot in the air'.

Developmental Stages 5 & 6

Finger and Thumb

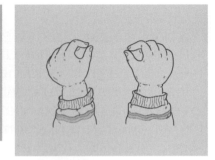

Aligning the first finger and thumb to touch, to make a hole or a circle is a key movement in developing grasp and in learning to use tools. The opposable thumb is a unique feature which only primates (humans and apes) have, and it helps them to pick up small objects, hold on to tools and eat with one hand.

Young babies (0-11 months)

Tiny babies won't be able to pick up small objects, but as they get more dextrous, they will be able to pick up smaller items. Start by offering small items of food such as peas, cooked pasta shapes or small pieces of carrot. Praise their efforts as they work to pick up these small items and put them in their mouths, first with a whole palm grip, but gradually with the pincer grip of finger and thumb.

Developmental Stage 1

Babies (8-20 months)

Continue to offer small finger food items, such as raisins, chopped vegetables, cooked spaghetti. Put small tins and other containers in treasure baskets. If these are transparent, babies can see small items hidden inside. Offer babies objects with small handles or textured play balls with projections to grip. Look for toys with holes, slits, or places to post things. Offer lots of containers for filling and emptying, and stacking toys of all sorts.

Developmental Stage 2

Young children (16-26 months)

Fine motor skills continue to develop, an letting go gently sometimes frustrates young children who are building, placing and balancing objects. Plenty of experience with good quality wooden bricks and simple construction sets will help. Pointing is a feature of early language development, when children are learning new words every hour. Pointing is a specific request – it means 'Tell me what that is called' – so learning to separate the index finger is crucial .

Developmental Stage 3

Children (22-40 months)

Lots of experience with small objects and smaller tools will build on children's growing dexterity. Decorate biscuits with small cake decorations and offer small items for collage and picture making. Provide thinner paint brushes and crayons alongside chunkier ones. Threading beads, spools or hollow pasta will help the co-ordination of both hands and separation of individual fingers. Construction toys such as Sticklebricks or Duplo will strengthen hand and finger muscles.

Developmental Stages 4 & 5

Older children (40-60+ months)

Provide scissors, pens, paint brushes and water, glue sticks, sequins and small beads – once children know about not eating small objects, the sky is the limit in using small obects and equipment! Some children will prefer smaller tools and mark making equipment such as scissors, fine felt pens, smaller pieces of paper, so add these to the range of equipment you offer. Make sure you have well made, child-sized equipment for gardening, cooking, home play and creative work.

Developmental Stages 5 & 6

Me and You

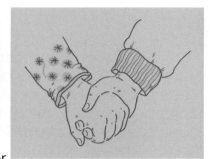

Working together to co-ordinate actions with an adult or a friend will help with movement and with the development of social skills. Lots of work in pairs, by finding and making up songs and rhymes, by using chants and raps, and by dances of all sorts will help to establish co-operative and collaborative movement.

Young babies (0-11 months)

Babies need to learn that they are separate beings with separate needs and opinions. This is a gradual process, that needs encouragement and attention from adults. Listening and watching carefully for messages from babies, through their movement, facial expression and the sounds they make will help you to understand them and will help them to realise that they can affect relationships with others.

Developmental Stage 1

Babies (8-20 months)

Long before babies can talk, they can get involved in activities with you. Their ways of communication are different, but just as powerful, and they certainly have minds of their own! Getting involved with them needs to be carefully handled, so you don't take over. Be a genuine partner in their self-chosen activities. Just be there and get involved if they seem to want you to – most babies love having some adult attention and company.

Developmental Stage 2

Young children (16-26 months)

Playing 'in parallel' is a feature of this age, but children will often let you echo what they are doing. If you want to do something together, it may be better to invite a child to come with you to a quiet place in your setting where you can sit and share a book and a rhyme, have a little teaparty with a teddy, or toss beanbags into a bucket together. Collaborative games are likely to be short lived at this stage, so be understanding when they get distracted and leave.

Developmental Stage 3

Children (22-40 months)

Maturity will make most children more amenable to working with you, and many will really enjoy paired activities when they get extra attention. Children of this age will enjoy going somewhere secret or secluded where you won't be disturbed – try dens and shelters, secluded corners of the garden or a curtained area for a game with one or two children, but make sure that every child gets a turn with you, playing a game, doing a puzzle, or even dancing.

Developmental Stages 4 & 5

Older children (40-60+ months)

By the time children are at the final stage of the EYFS, they will be in larger groups and will need to learn how to play and work in pairs and groups, with or without an adult. Focus on particular interests or skills they may need to practise. Invite them to play a card or number game, do a more complex jigsaw, make a special card, join in cooking, or prepare a new role play area. Working in a small group develops social skills and concentration.

Developmental Stages 5 & 6

If you find this book useful you might also like to look at ...

97814081125540

9781408112434

9781905019588

9781906029012

All available from acblack.com/featherstone